Play
Money

Tana Reiff

A Pacemaker **LifeTimes™ 2** Book

GLOBE PEARSON

Pearson Learning Group

LifeTimes™2 Titles

Take Away Three
Climbing the Wall
The Door Is Open
Just for Today
Chicken by Che
Play Money
The Missing Piece

Cover Illustration: Arthur Koch

ISBN 0-8224-4607-3
Printed in the United States of America

6 7 8 9 10   07 06 05 04 03

Globe
Fearon

Pearson Learning Group

1-800-321-3106
www.pearsonlearning.com

Contents

CHAPTER 1

There was a knock
on the door.
Connie got up
from her chair
to answer it.

"Hi," said the friendly face
at the door.
"My name is Brett.
I'm your neighbor
across the hall."

"Nice to meet you,"
said Connie.
"My name is Connie.
Come on in.
You're the first person
to visit me
in my new apartment."

Connie and Brett
got along right away.
Brett was easy
to talk to.
He seemed
like an old friend.

"I work
at the radio station,"
Connie told him.
"I work
in the office."

"Do you have
a husband?"
Brett asked her.

"I did,"
she said.
"We broke up.
I'm on my own now.
I'm doing OK.
I get a check
from my job

every week.
All I need
is a credit card.
I don't always have
money for things
when I need them."

Brett said
she should get a card
from a store.
If she paid her bills
on time,
she could get
a major credit card
from a bank.

So the next day
Connie went
to Strong's.
It was
her favorite store.
She filled out
a paper
to get a credit card.

A week later
she got some mail
from Strong's.
She ran over
to Brett's apartment.
"Look at this!"
she said.
"I got my card!"

Together they went
down to Strong's.
Connie bought herself
a beautiful pair of shoes.
"This is like having
play money!"
she laughed.

"You *will*
get a bill,
you know,"
said Brett.

Thinking It Over

1. Have you ever met someone
    you got along with
    right away?

2. Do you think credit cards
    are a good idea?

3. Why do you think
    Connie didn't already
    have credit?

CHAPTER 2

For the first time
Connie was in control
of her own money.
She had married young.
She worked
while she was married.
But her husband
had handled all their money.

Now, Connie could spend
her money
the way she wanted to.
If she didn't
have the cash,
she used her credit card.

"I'm having such fun!"
she told Brett.
"I can buy
anything I want!"

"Do you
really believe that?"
Brett asked.

"Don't worry,"
said Connie.
"I pay my bills
every month
on time.
I even pay
in full.
That way,
I don't pay
any interest."

"Sounds good,"
said Brett.
"I guess you know
what you're doing."

The radio station
was near the bank.
Connie stopped there
after work

the next day.
She wanted
a bank credit card
she could use anywhere.

The man at the bank
made some phone calls.
"Your credit is good,"
he told Connie.
"We can give you
a credit card.
It will be good
for up to $500."

He explained
how the card works.
Connie would get a bill
each month.
She must pay
a small amount
each time.
She will owe interest
on the amount
she doesn't pay.

"It sounds
pretty simple,"
Connie said.

"It is simple,"
explained the man.
"We want to make buying
as easy as possible."

Thinking It Over

1. When two people are married, who should handle the money?

2. How does a bank or store check your credit?

3. Do you think it's too easy to buy on credit?

CHAPTER 3

Connie got
her new bank card.
She took Brett
out to dinner.
She paid for dinner
with the card.

Soon Connie began
to get letters
from banks
all over the country.
"We'll give you
a credit line
of $1,000!"
said one letter.
"Just sign your name."

"Why not?"
Connie said to herself.
She signed her name
for three more cards

from three more banks.
However, she had to pay
for each card.
The costs were adding up.

Connie began
to buy everything
with credit cards.
She used a card
for new clothes.
Now she had more clothes
than she could wear.

"Are you rich
or something?"
Brett asked her.
"You're getting
a little carried away.
Those cards
aren't play money,
you know."

"That's my problem,
not yours,"
Connie told him.

"I'm speaking up
because I care
about you,"
said Brett.
"I don't want
to see you
get into money trouble."

"Really, Brett,"
said Connie.
"It's none
of your business."

Thinking It Over

1. How can one decide
    what to buy on credit
    and what to pay for
    on the spot?

2. How can credit cards
    be like play money?

3. Would you tell a friend
    he or she was in trouble?

CHAPTER 4

Connie's credit card bills
came faster and faster.
If a bill asked
for a low of $10,
that's all
Connie paid.
She couldn't keep up
with all the bills.
The interest
built up more and more.
Connie was getting
in over her head.

One night
Connie and Brett
were watching TV.
An ad came on
for a credit card company.
A man and woman
were flying
around the world.

They were having
a great time.

"That's you,"
Brett said to Connie.
"Pretty soon
you'll be flying
around the world
with your play money.
But how will you
pay the bills?"

"Stop it,"
Connie said.
She knew
she was running
into money trouble.
But she didn't
want Brett
to know he was right.

Thinking It Over

1. Do you ever see yourself
    in TV ads? How?

2. Do you think TV ads
    get us to buy things
    we don't need?

3. Is it hard for you
    to tell someone
    you were wrong?

CHAPTER 5

Connie didn't stop
using her credit cards.
Instead, she used them
more often.
She brought home
more clothes.
She hadn't paid
for the other ones yet.

Connie also brought home
things for the apartment.
She didn't need
a new clock.
But she got one.
She didn't need
a clothes tree, either.
But she got one.

Connie didn't like
many of the things she bought.

But she didn't
return them.
She just kept on
buying things.

Connie also got
presents for Brett
and for her parents.

When the bills came,
she didn't even open them.
She didn't want to see
how much money
she didn't have.

Thinking It Over

1.   Would you return something
     you didn't like?

2.   Do you think Connie feels
     as if everything is free?

3.   What would you do
     with bills you couldn't pay?

CHAPTER 6

Some of Connie's cards
let her spend
up to $500.
Some let her spend
up to $1,000.
One card
let her spend
up to $2,000.
Before too long
Connie had spent
all she could
on most of the cards.
And the bills
kept piling up.

Connie needed
to get away
from all the bills.
She needed
a vacation.

The radio station
gave her time off.
But she didn't have
enough money.

Then she learned
a new trick.
She learned
that she could get money
from a credit card.
She went
to the bank
that handled
one of the cards.
She asked for $300.
They gave it to her,
just like that!
The amount was
added to her bill
for that card.

Connie packed
a few things.
She filled her car

with gas.
She drove all day.

   That night,
Connie stopped
at a motel.
When she woke up
the next morning,
she wasn't even sure
where she was.

   That day Connie drove north
until she came
to the mountains.
When it got dark,
she turned around
and headed for home.
It wasn't much
of a vacation.

Thinking It Over

1. Why did Connie
    get so mixed up
    on her trip?

2. Do you think Connie
    learned anything
    from the trip?

3. Did you ever go somewhere
    without knowing
    where you were going?

CHAPTER 7

After dinner
Brett came over
to say hello.
"Welcome home!"
he said.
"I didn't know
you were going away."

"I don't
have to tell you everything,"
said Connie.

"No problem,"
said Brett.
"Where did you go?"

"I don't know,"
said Connie.

"OK, don't tell me,"
said Brett.

"No, I really
don't know,"
said Connie.
"Brett, I have
to tell you something.
I've got money trouble.
Real bad money trouble."

"Why don't you stop
using your credit cards?"
Brett asked.

Connie didn't
hear him.
Or she didn't want
to hear him.

Soon the phone calls started.
Stores and banks
called Connie
at the radio station.
They asked
when they would get
some money from her.

"You are getting
too many phone calls
at work,"
Connie's boss told her.
"This is work time!"

"I didn't tell them
to call me here,"
Connie said.

"The calls
must stop,"
said the boss.
"If they don't,
I'll have to fire you."

"The calls
will stop,"
said Connie.
When the boss walked away,
Connie began to cry.
She hoped
no one saw her.

Thinking It Over

1. Why did Connie
    tell Brett at last
    that she was in trouble?

2. Should people call you at work
    for money?

3. Should you be able
    to talk to anyone you wish to
    while you're at work?

CHAPTER 8

The phone calls
at work
didn't stop.
One of the callers
was a very nice woman
from the bank.
Her name
was Mrs. Block.

"Connie," she said.
"Why don't you
come to my office?
We can have
a nice talk.
We can try
to work out
your money problems."

Connie felt ready
to talk.

"OK," she said.
"I'll come in tomorrow."

The next day
Connie went
to see Mrs. Block.
"I know you can't
pay off your bills
all at once,"
said Mrs. Block.
"But you must
open your mail.
If the bill
asks for a low of $10
you must try
to pay $10.
That will keep you
out of trouble
with the bank."

"I know you're right,"
said Connie.
"I'm so afraid.
I'm afraid
I'll never get out
of this hole."

"You'll get out,"
said Mrs. Block.
"Just don't dig yourself in
any deeper."

Then Mrs. Block
had another idea.
She gave Connie
the name of a budget counseling
office.
"It doesn't cost anything,"
Mrs. Block explained.
"The counselor
will go over all your bills.
Together you'll decide
how to handle things."

"Where is this place?"
Connie asked.
"I want to go right now."

The counseling office
was only a few blocks away.
Connie went there
as soon as she left
the bank.

Connie walked
into the office.
The first person she saw
was a very good-looking man.
"Come on in,"
he said to her.
"My name is David.
Now don't worry.
We're going to work out
your problem together."

That sounded
very interesting
to Connie.
In fact,
David sounded
very interesting
to Connie.

Thinking It Over

1. Have you ever dug yourself
   into a deep hole?

2. Why do you think Connie
   went to the budget counselor
   right away?

3. Do you think it matters
   whether or not
   David is good-looking?

CHAPTER 9

Together, David and Connie
studied Connie's money problems.
David wrote down
how much money
Connie made each week.
Then he wrote down
how much money
she had to pay out.

"You must pay
what the bill
asks for,"
David told Connie.
"But you'll never
get ahead that way.
So you have to try
to pay more
than the bill asks for."

"But I don't have
enough money,"
said Connie.

"Then how
could you cut back
on the things you buy?"
asked David.

"I guess
I'll have to buy
only what I really need,"
said Connie.
"And I won't pay
for anything
with play money anymore."

David laughed.
"Play money?"
he asked.

"That's what
my friend Brett and I
call my credit cards,"
said Connie.

"Suppose you needed something
and didn't have the money,"
said David.
"Would you use your cards?"

"No way,"
said Connie.
"I'll only use
cold, green money."
She pulled
a pile of credit cards
out of her bag.
One by one
she cut every card
in half.
Then she threw them away.
"Now I know
I won't use
my credit cards,"
she laughed.

David laughed, too.
"I want you
to come see me
once a week,"
he said.
"And I want you
to think of more ways
to cut down on
what you spend.

You want to pay off
those bills."

"I'll think
about how to cut down,"
said Connie.
"And I'll see you
next week."
That was fine
with Connie.
She wouldn't mind
seeing this man anytime.
She would remember his eyes
all week.

Thinking It Over

1.   Was it a good idea
     for Connie
     to cut up her cards?

2.   How would you cut down
     on what you spend?

3.   How can you tell
     David likes Connie, too?

CHAPTER 10

The next week
Connie went back
to see David.

"I decided
how I can
cut down on
what I spend,"
she told him.
"I'm going to move back
with my mom and dad.
I'll pay some rent
to them.
But I will still save
a lot of money."

"I must say,
that's a good idea,"
said David.
"Paying less rent

should help you
pay off those bills
a lot faster."

Connie and David went over
the credit card bills
that had come in that week.
They worked out
how much to pay
on each one.

When they were finished,
David looked Connie
in the eye.
"How do you feel
about mixing business
with fun?"
he asked her.

"I don't know,"
said Connie.
"What do you mean?"

"I mean
would you like

to go out with me?"
asked David.

That question
was music to Connie's ears.
But she didn't know
whether she should say
yes or no.
"I'm not sure,"
she said.
"You know
I don't have
any money."

"That's OK,"
said David.
"This one is on me."

"Well, then, sure,"
said Connie.
"I'd love to go out
with you."

"How's Saturday night?"
asked David.

"It's fine,"
said Connie.

"We can talk
about anything at all,"
said David.
"But let's not talk
about money."

"Fine with me,"
said Connie.
"See you Saturday."

Thinking It Over

1. Do you think
    it's hard for Connie
    to move back
    with her parents?

2. Is it ever OK
    to mix business with fun?

3. Who should pay for dates—
    the man or the woman?

CHAPTER 11

When Connie got home
she stopped in
to see Brett.
She told him
she would be moving.

Brett didn't like
that news.
"Who gave you
that bad idea?"
he asked.

"It was *my* idea,"
said Connie.
"And it's a good idea.
My budget counselor
asked me to think
of ways to cut down
on what I spend.

I have to pay off
all those bills."

"Is this
the good-looking
one named David?"
asked Brett.
"I don't think
I like him."

"David's really nice,"
said Connie.
"In fact,
I'm going out with him
Saturday night."

"Oh, really?"
said Brett.
"I told you long ago
to be careful
with those credit cards.
Why didn't you
listen to *me?*
Besides, I really love you!"

"I'm sorry,"
said Connie.
"All this time
I thought that
we were just good friends."

"Just friends?"
asked Brett.

"You mean
a lot to me,"
said Connie.
"I never wanted
to hurt you.
You're my best friend."

Thinking It Over

1. Why didn't Connie
    listen to Brett long ago
    about the credit cards?

2. Did you ever have a friend
    who looked at you
    as more than a friend?

CHAPTER 12

Connie and David
went out to dinner.
They ate
at a very nice little place
with a view of the water.
They didn't talk
about money.

However, Connie
was thinking
about money.
She ordered
the dinner
with the lowest price.
These days
she always looked
at prices first.

She and David
had lots to talk about.
David had been married

before, too.
He had been
on his own
for two years.

"Not being married
isn't so bad,"
said Connie.
"But you have to watch—"
She didn't finish
her sentence.

"I know
what you were going to say,"
said David.
"But the fact is
you have to watch
your money matters
when you're married, too.
I see many married people
with money problems."

Connie smiled.
David was
an understanding man.

"You know something?"
she said.
"You're very right
for your job."

They looked out
at the water.
It was like
a sheet of glass.

Connie and David
saw each other
three more times
during the next week.
Two of those times
were not in David's office.

Thinking It Over

1. What does
    the last sentence mean?

2. What people do you know
    who are right for their jobs?

3. How important is it
    to look at prices first?

CHAPTER 13

Brett knocked
on Connie's door.

"Come on in,"
said Connie.
"Are you still
angry with me?"

"I just wondered
if you needed help
with your move,"
Brett said.

"I could use
some help,"
said Connie.
"But I don't
expect you
to help me."

"Oh," said Brett.
"I should know better.
Is David helping?"

"No," said Connie.
"As a matter of fact,
he's not."

"Well, I can get
my friend's truck,"
said Brett.
"We can do it
next Saturday.
It won't take long.
And after we're finished,
you just run along
and go out with David."

"Must you be smart
about it?"
Connie asked.

"I'm not being smart,"
said Brett.

"I mean it.
I can't be angry with you.
So you're not
in love with me.
I wouldn't want
to miss out
on a good friend."

"Then let's be friends,"
said Connie.

"OK," said Brett.
"I'll have the truck here
first thing Saturday morning."

"Brett," said Connie,
"you're a good sport."

Thinking It Over

1.   How is Brett
     showing he is a good friend?

2.   What are some things
     a person has to do
     to get ready to move?

3.   What's another way
     a person can be
     a good sport?

CHAPTER 14

Connie moved back
with her parents.
She got along fine
with them.
But she planned
to move back out
in a year.

She kept her job
at the radio station.
The banks and stores
stopped calling her.
She was paying off
her bills.

And Connie stopped
each card
as soon as
she paid it off.

She saw David often.
The more she knew him,

the more she liked him.
He felt the same way
about her.

Connie also saw Brett
now and then.
He had a new girlfriend
named Page.
Connie met her
and liked her.
Page and Brett
seemed cut out
for each other.
Connie was very happy
about that.

Connie's money troubles
got better every week.
But sometimes
she felt the need
for a credit card.

David was still
Connie's budget counselor.
He said she might want
just one card.

He said
that some bank cards
have lower interest
than others.
He gave her a list
of the banks
with the lowest interest.

Connie shopped around
the banks.
Some banks
wanted her
to pay for a card.
At some banks
she would not have to pay.
She found a bank
where she didn't have to pay.
It also had
the lowest interest.
Now that her credit was better,
the bank gave her
a credit card.

Soon the card
came in the mail.
Connie wanted to use it

just once.
She called
a flower shop.
She ordered flowers
to be sent
to Brett.
"Thanks for everything,"
said the note.
"Love, Connie."

Then she put the card
in the back
of her desk drawer.
"I'll save it
for a rainy day,"
she told herself.

Now she saw
that the sun was shining.
And the phone
was ringing.
It must be David.

Thinking It Over

1.   Do you think
     Connie is on the right track?
     Why or why not?

2.   Do you think
     a person like Connie
     should have a credit card?

3.   Why did Connie
     send flowers to Brett?

4.   What are you saving
     for "a rainy day"?